BECOMING A DIAMOND

THE STRONGEST, MOST VALUABLE VERSION OF YOU

Sivad Johnson

Foreword by Eboni T. Thomas

Copyright © 2021 Sivad Johnson & Eboni T. Thomas

All rights reserved. No part of this book may be reproduced or transmitted in any form or by any means without written permission from the author. Contact: info@sivadiam.com.

T.A.L.K. Publishing
5215 North Ironwood Road, Suite 200
Glendale, WI 53217
talkconsulting.net

T.A.L.K.
Publishing
TELL. ACCEPT. LEARN. KNOW.
talkconsulting.net

Title: Becoming A Diamond
Subtitle: The Strongest, Most Valuable Version of You
ISBN: 978-1-952327-34-6
Library of Congress Control Number: 2021900167

This book is not meant to be used, nor should it be used, to diagnose or treat any medical condition or mental health illness. This book details the author's personal experiences with and opinions about self-development practices. We do not recommend trying the practice of cold exposure or any other examples of what the author has done and shared in this book without consulting with your physician and seeking medical advice. Neither the author or publisher, nor any coauthors, editors, contributors, or other representatives will be liable for damages arising out of or in connection with the use of this book.

This book is dedicated to
the daughters of Sivad Johnson,
Kyndall Sirrah and Hayden Skye.
May the legacy of his life continue
to make a positive ripple
effect around the
world.

CONTENTS

About The Author 9
Foreword 11
Acknowledgments 17
Introduction 19
Chapter 1: In The Rough 21
   Defining Thoughts: Admitting What Is 29
Chapter 2: Clarity 35
   Refining Thoughts: Defining What's Desired 37
   DIAMOND EVOLUTION: Phase 1 39
   Writing Your Visions Into Actions 40
Chapter 3: In The Dark 43
   Defining Thoughts: Seeing Your Choices Clearly 48
Chapter 4: Choice 53
   Refining Thoughts: Navigating Life's Mazes 55
   DIAMOND EVOLUTION: Phase 2 56
   Writing Your Visions Into Actions 57
Chapter 5: In The Making 61
   Defining Thoughts: Pushing Through The Fire 66
Chapter 6: Commitment 73
   Refining Thoughts: Committing To Be All You Can ... 74

DIAMOND EVOLUTION: Phase 3 76
Writing Yourr Visions Intro Actions 77
Chapter 7: In The Light 81
Defining Thoughts: Doing The Work - Repeatedly 84
Chapter 8: Consistency 87
Refining Thoughts: Being Consistent For Growth 89
DIAMOND EVOLUTION: Phase 4 93
Writing Your Visions into Actions 94
Chapter 9: In Conclusion 97
Notes 99

ABOUT THE AUTHOR

Sivad Johnson was a public speaker, gifted artist, and loving father of two. He appeared on stage at events for The Moth, a New York-based nonprofit group dedicated to the art and craft of storytelling. His theme-based stories took him to The Moth GrandSLAM and Mainstage. He was featured nationally on The Moth Radio Hour as well. As a keynote, panelist, and member of Toastmasters International, he spoke to youth groups, students, and adults. He also shared inspirational messages on T-shirt and clothing designs and YouTube.

A Detroit native and 26-year veteran of the Detroit Fire Department, Sivad followed in his father's footsteps when becoming a firefighter in 1994. Promoted to sergeant on September 20, 2016, he earned numerous citations throughout his career, including the 2017 Detroit Public Safety Foundation's Above & Beyond Awards Medal of Valor for his acts of bravery and heroism while in the line of duty.

On August 21, 2020, Sivad gave his life bravely by diving into the Detroit River while off duty to help rescue three young girls who were struggling. His ultimate sacrifice, a heroic team effort with other civilians, made international headlines.

The City of Detroit honored him with a memorial service, unveiling a new fire and rescue boat named for him. The City Council of Detroit honored him with a Spirit of Detroit Award for exceptional achievement, outstanding leadership, and dedication to improving the quality of life.

In 2020, the Detroit Public Safety Foundation posthumously awarded Sivad its Purple Heart at the Above & Beyond Awards ceremony. This award is presented to firefighters, police officers, and emergency medical technicians who are injured or killed in the performance of their duties while exhibiting exceptional bravery in unusual circumstances.

The Trump administration sent a letter of condolences to Sivad's family from The White House recognizing his "courage and selflessness" to protect and help others as representing "the best of America."

FOREWORD

My brother, Sivad Heshimu Johnson, believed in getting the most out of this experience called life. He believed in the BIBLE: Basic Instructions Before Leaving Earth. He believed in investing quality time with those he loved, and he had a passion for serving and protecting others. Allow me to share more of who he was by starting with ...

His Heritage

When my brother was born, our parents gave him a name that would honor his heritage and foretell a future of significance. As his younger sister, I grew to understand and appreciate the origin and meaning of his name.

Sivad's first name, pronounced sĭ-VAHD, is our mother Reada's maiden name spelled backward: Davis became Sivad. He mirrored her values and beliefs as he grew up in a Christian household, and he inherited her love for poetic words.

His middle name, Heshimu, is a Swahili word that translates to respect, honor, or courage. Our parents believed it meant "brave young warrior" when they welcomed him into the world on September 5, 1970, in Detroit, Michigan.

His last name is our father's: Johnson. William (Bill) R. Johnson served as a US Army combat medic in Vietnam and as a Detroit firefighter for 20 years, modeling the values of service and courage. Our younger brother, Jamal, also became a firefighter, confronting the risks inherent in saving and serving others. Gifted with speaking, acting, modeling and carpentry, Jamal has appeared in films and on "This Old House." His supporting role in caring for Sivad's daughters has become major.

A Hero

Many refer to Sivad as a "superman" and a hero. For many years, he ran into burning buildings exceeding 600 degrees. Ever the adventure-seeker, he leaped out of a flying plane on a bucket-list skydiving adventure. He completed two Tough Mudder endurance events, featuring up to 25 obstacle courses. He was strong enough to endure cold exposure, taking cold showers at 5 o'clock every morning to gain clarity and focus.

Clearly, the world sees and recognizes Sivad for his ultimate heroic act, sacrificing his life to help save three, which caused a tremendous ripple effect. Our family believes it's no coincidence that a 3.2 magnitude earthquake occurred near Detroit Beach around the same time he entered the Detroit River.

A Giant

Sivad was a handsome "giant" who stood an impressive 6 feet 3 inches tall and magnetically drew eyes and people to him wherever he entered a room. Height commands attention regardless of who has it, but it does not convey character. In Sivad, there was an inevitable melding of the two because he was "larger than life" in so many ways.

He was big on living out his values of service and dedication. One of his mottos was "Bravely do or bravely die!" He had a colossal heart for people, most especially his daughters, Kyndall and Hayden, and his ex-wife, Suzette. He unabashedly stated that his girls were his reason for being.

He had a special passion for the town in which he lived. His love for the City of Detroit nurtured his team spirit, leading him to design fashions that extolled its virtues. His commitment to the betterment of the city extended to the community and the world.

A Gift

Sivad was a gift and he was gifted. His artistic vision was evident before he was four years old, as he could draw remarkable likenesses of the Volkswagen Beetle our parents owned. He honed those skills to perfection, creating lasting works of art across many genres, which many people purchased and enjoyed.

His was a gift of compassionate communication. Sivad had the uncanny ability to see with an inner eye and hear with a third ear. Almost everyone he knew came to him at some point seeking his wise counsel, focused attention, or simple help. And they came away feeling like they got just what they needed. He anticipated and responded to every request he possibly could.

His TIME

The week before Sivad's earthly departure, he and his daughters visited me and my family in Georgia. A dual goal for the trip was to have me begin editing this book, which he had just completed writing, while investing quality time. He often said, "This Instant Means Everything"— the phrase he coined, turning the word TIME into an acronym.

We engaged in deep conversations about life and purpose, as always. I watched Sivad meditating each morning under a tree and marveled at his daily routines. I witnessed him show love and give undivided attention to each of his daughters—hugs of comfort and of pride, individual talks and outdoor walks, firm negotiations on food indulgences and activity requests—tailored to their ages, 17 and 10 at the time.

Our kids enjoyed plenty of cousin time playing card games, building indoor forts, fishing, blowing bubbles, and drawing with sidewalk chalk. We gathered around the table for meals. We laughed. We embraced. We started reading through what he had written for this book. But mostly, we just cherished those five days together.

After Sivad returned to Detroit, we exchanged text messages expressing how much we enjoyed the time we were afforded to invest in each other. Little did I know how bittersweet and invaluable that investment would become. I am beyond honored and humbled that God chose me to receive the baton from Sivad in the form of this completed writing he left in my care. I refrained from making extensive edits in order to keep this book authentic to Sivad's voice and message. He even conceptualized the cover design.

It has been said that the present is a gift. Sivad was present and remains present—our gift of love that we open each day with gratitude, respect, and honor. May what he speaks through this book be a gift to you and yours.

—Eboni T. Thomas, editor and Sivad's sister

More About the Author's Sister & Editor

Eboni T. (Johnson) Thomas is a freelance editor and writer for *Savoy* magazine. She started her journalism career as a real estate reporter for the *Detroit Free Press*. She moved to Georgia in 1999 and served briefly as a freelance writer for the Sunday "Homefinder" section of *The Atlanta Journal-Constitution*.

For eight years, she developed corporate communications and marketing materials for Ernst & Young (EY) as a writer, copy editor, and proofreader. As a contractor, she has engaged in a variety of editorial projects, including business and career profiles for *Connect*, EY's alumni magazine.

Born and raised in Detroit, Michigan, Eboni discovered her love for writing at an early age. She earned a BA in Communications from the University of Detroit-Mercy, where she studied journalism, marketing, public relations, TV/radio broadcasting, and some architecture.

Sivad & Jamal in their father Bill's fire gear (left photo); Sivad & Eboni (top center) Eboni, Sivad & Jamal (bottom center); Sivad & Jamal in their tire uniforms (right)

ACKNOWLEDGMENTS

There are so many I attribute to my knowledge seeking, interest sparking, strength building, and movement inspiring. Many were family, friends, and coworkers. Some were strangers who engaged with me in one-time conversations.

Others were individuals I've never met in person, but rather by way of media, such as books, videos, movies, and seminars.

Without a doubt, I absolutely give credit to the Source of all creation for making this all possible within me. I am a product of this all, and I am eternally thankful. Blessings to you.

—Sivad Johnson

INTRODUCTION

Becoming A Diamond: The Strongest, Most Valuable Version of You is an inspirational, self-development book for those seeking to find greater purpose in life and to make the most of their time here on earth. Through reflections from author Sivad Johnson's dynamic life and career of service, you will journey with him from one of his early jobs into his heart for art, through his dedication to fighting fires and saving lives to his remarkable practices of self-discipline.

The book outlines steps for you to evolve into a metaphorical diamond while trekking through life's labyrinth of decisions. It serves up *defining* and *refining* thoughts alternately in chapters that help you honestly face (and own) where you are now and clearly define where you want to be in the future. The author delineates the phases in an actual diamond's evolution and parallels them with visions for you to put into action personally on your path to becoming the strongest, most valuable version of yourself.

As you read this book, you will note the content alternates between the author's presentation of thought-provoking concepts and storytelling from his own experiences. The interplay of chapters introduces and defines his thoughts with flashbacks to different points in his life. You will discover the "four C's" to becoming a diamond as the author refines his thoughts on life's circumstances. You'll find practical exercises to apply the principles to positively transform your outlook on life and set and reach your goals. The book concludes with the author's final thoughts and personal salute for your journey.

Ready to start becoming a diamond?

Let's roll ...

CHAPTER 1

IN THE ROUGH

A piece of carbon is the precursor to a diamond. Carbon is the fourth most abundant element in the world. It is part of more than 10 million compounds and as such is known as the "element of life." You are carbon, at least in some portion of your makeup. Admitted or not, it is the truth. Truth is clarity. Like a piece of buried carbon, you may find yourself in darkness in life. You, too, may be exposed to heat and pressure, perhaps extreme, for who knows how long. You might not like, or you might even hate, your current state. This can be the place where your strengthening begins. Admit where you are, but don't plan on staying here.

As both the material and the maker, you hold the ability to create, then live the existence you desire. Can you picture yourself being an incredibly strong, brightly shining, extremely valuable diamond? Can you envision the world seeing you and being in awe of what you've become? If not that far, can you visualize being a diamond in the rough? You or others recognize your potential. You welcome the challenge and are willing to invest more time and work at moving yourself forward. What do you think of that, and how does it feel?

Still too far? How about seeing yourself peeking out from what mostly encases you, exposing just enough to see a ray of light shining on you. Not there? Okay, try something smaller. Just picture yourself not being under the constant pressure, darkness, and heat—the extremely uncomfortable environment that began your transformation. Just picture the slightest easing, some minute breathing room. Or you can practice focusing only on your current state. You know precisely what this feels like. Two pictures, two options: here or somewhere different and better.

***

Life is unpredictable. Throughout our lifetimes, we find ourselves in different situations. Some we enjoy experiencing, while we hate to be in others. Many situations are unexpected, not of our conscious choosing or control. Now, regardless of what situation we may find ourselves in or what means put us there, we can do something. But there needs to be an admission. Neither wanting not to be in a situation nor avoiding a decision will make the situation simply go away.

As a responsible adult, gone should be our childlike ways of hiding behind cupped hands over our eyes or drawing a blanket over our heads, wishing we weren't where we are. We cannot expect the act of sticking a finger in each ear while verbalizing *La, la, la, I can't hear you* or *There's no place like home* to rid ourselves from facing what is. If we won't look crystal clearly at where we are for what it is, how then can we take even the slightest action toward positioning ourselves somewhere better than the present?

I'm not saying it will be pleasant to seek, find, and admit to what is. In fact, it may be ugly, very painful, or quite embarrassing. But it is absolutely necessary. Taking all blinders off allows us to see a base to build upon—a base of truth. As Canadian psychologist Dr. Jordan Peterson, whom I respect for his matter-of-fact understanding and delivery, has said, "... there is nothing more powerful"[1] than truth. That's gospel to me, and I love it. I haven't always wanted or practiced seeking such truth.

Admittedly, I did my fair share of squinting at my own reality. Subsequently, that reality suffered. I suffered, and others I cared for suffered. When I started getting really tired of it was when I was willing to take a true look at things. I eventually adopted and, hesitantly, put *honestly facing reality* into play, and it began to affect life. Practicing it changed my life for the better. I'll never go back to turning a blind eye or donning rose-colored glasses. I seek twenty-twenty vision in all matters concerning me. In hindsight, I think my vision began to improve early on when I was working a mundane job and I knew I could do more.

One morning, I woke up late and looked around my room. It was my third day off during a week-long vacation I'd earned while working for a local steakhouse. My job title at the restaurant was host. I would greet and seat the patrons who came in to dine. I'd check to see if they had reservations, then pick an appropriate, available seat for them. The customer interactions were most often pleasant.

I wasn't much of an extrovert, but neither was I afraid to talk with people, so I was comfortable enough to do my job with a smile. Sometimes I had to try and soothe the rarely encountered impatient or upset customer. I usually did so in a calm manner. It was okay work for the money. I would get a small cut from the pooled tips of the waitstaff at the end of the shift.

All in all, it was just enough money for me, at 19, to pay for my social activities, keep my eight-year-old car on the road, and give my mom a portion as a contribution to living at home still. I don't think she needed it, but she was teaching me one of those all-important life lessons. I hadn't taken my high school experience seriously enough, so I ended up graduating from summer school. That was super embarrassing.

I attended a semester or two at a local community college. I thought that was what you do after leaving high school. But I messed that over enough that my parents pulled the plug on paying for it. In my senior year of high school, a recruiter pursued me to join the armed forces, which my dad had done. I didn't want that. So, I was doing the last of the three options my parents had given me: go to school, go to the military, or go to work. I respected that.

Honestly, during that time off, I chilled at home mostly or met up with some friends when they were free. We'd usually hang out in Detroit or one of the surrounding cities. I was scheduled to be on vacation for five days, then off through the weekend, which meant I would have to be back at work on Monday. Something about that realization sparked a small thought within me. Maybe it was initiated after watching some cartoons on TV, reading some comic books, or something else. But I thought, "Dang, wouldn't it be sweet to make money by drawing, instead of working in a restaurant?"

I did have natural artistic talent, like my dad and uncle. I would often choose to draw during my free time. Being on punishment in my younger years wasn't so bad either, until my parents got hip to me being too content in my room's solitude. They'd take away my art supplies. I had even taken drafting and commercial art classes all through high school. I practiced drawing superheroes and mimicked Disney animated character styles. I even illustrated some automotive designs of vehicles I thought I'd like to see on the road someday. But none of those careers seemed possible to me, especially without taking the proper college courses somewhere.

The next day, I started feeling that I really didn't want to go back to the steakhouse. But how could I get a job drawing for money—where and for whom? I thought, *Wait a minute, what about doing the designs for T-shirts and stuff?* I figured someone had to create the art that got printed, whether for big brands like Nike and Adidas or even the local businesses, school teams, family reunions, social clubs, etc. The more I thought about it, the more I realized something: If I didn't do something to change it, I'd have to go back to the restaurant and pick back up with what I was doing.

I started thinking about sitting at a table—or better yet, an art desk—drawing all kinds of different, interesting things and being paid for it. As I continued those thoughts, the clearer the visualization became. As I persisted, a feeling started growing. No more slacks and ties. No more listening to the dinner music that looped so much I grew to know which songs would play in sequence, whether I liked them or not. That painted a clearer picture also—one resulting in a growing, negative feeling. I decided I'd better at least see if I could get hired somehow, someway, using my drawing skills.

I looked up about eight to ten screen printing shops nearby and not too far away. I wrote their addresses and phone numbers on a piece of paper. I grabbed a portfolio I had and filled it with some of my best work from high school and things I drew at home during my down times. I opted for clean, dark jeans with a polo-style shirt for this job hunt instead of the slacks, shirt, and tie choice (as my parents taught me for formal job interviews) I'd normally wear. I picked the closest place to my home to stop by first. I walked in and introduced myself, inquired about how they produced their artwork, and presented my work. *No bite. Okay, on to the next.*

Business after business, I stepped in smiling, speaking, showing, asking—but none were interested enough to hire me. Scratched another and another off my list. It was growing shorter. I was growing hungry. I had already hit the farthest locations out I had planned to hit, that day, at least. I stopped to grab a bite and figured I'd hit two more on my way back home. Then, my plan would be to write down the next ones for tomorrow.

One of them was closed, so I scratched that off. *I'll hit the next one and then call it a day,* I thought. This one was about ten minutes from my home in Detroit, in the neighboring city of Redford: Integrity

Screen Printers. I parked at the small, white building and walked in. A woman at the counter greeted me. I inquired about how they created their artwork and asked if someone would take a look at mine to consider hiring me for that task. She told me to hold on while she went to get one of the owners.

A gentleman came from the back. He greeted me and asked me to repeat what I was offering. So, I did. He said they already had a full-time, in-house artist, but my work looked pretty good and he had an idea. He grabbed the other owner to come up front, and they both looked at my portfolio.

I didn't know what to think at that point. Then, they opened a door behind a different counter and asked another gentleman to come take a look. I saw him get up from a drawing table and walk into the main room. I assumed this must be their in-house artist. He flipped through my portfolio. One of the owners said, "He's looking to get a job here. He'd like to do some art for us. Jim, what do you think?"

Jim responded nonchalantly, "I think you should hire him."

DEFINING THOUGHTS:
Admitting What Is

I believe that if we don't, or won't, look with absolute honesty at what is, then we'll be incapable to clearly picture anything better for ourselves. It's best not to pretend like you don't know what situation you're in. If you actually don't know, once you do, admit it, at least to yourself if no one else. You truly don't have to admit it to anyone else. But by being this honest with yourself, you take the first step toward making anything different or better than it is.

It serves no one any purpose to stay in a state of pulling the wool over their own eyes. Let me be crystal clear. Admitting what is should not make you feel negatively or get into any sort of a rut. There is no reason for you to stay there, especially if it maintains or increases any ill feelings or disables you within any dangerous situation.

The sole purpose is just to know where you are—and own it. This will be your launchpad to that which is better.

Many times, our brains do the amazingly swift calculations of recognizing and alerting our bodies to what isn't good for us. Have you ever touched something extremely hot? In milliseconds, you had clarity of that. You thought of a better place for your hand to be, then pulled it away. Something bad to something better. Done. Thank goodness for that, lest we might have fingers and hands that resembled cooked pieces of bacon.

Mmm, bacon. Wait, would that really be a tragedy? Pardon me, I digress.

***

The owners of the screen print business thanked Jim for his opinion, and he went back to his work. They left the room briefly, then returned. One looked at me and asked, "When can you start?"

Internally, I thought, *What! Are they serious, just like that?* Vocally, I replied, "Monday!" Then I clarified that I actually had to go in to work Monday, but I'd put in my notice to terminate when I did. I shook both of their hands, verbalized a thank you, and walked out.

I beamed. *You did it, Sivad! You made it happen!* I rushed home to tell my mom. She congratulated me, and I felt super proud.

I began working at the screen print shop a couple of weeks later, but not in the way I thought. They told me I would help with overflow artwork if Jim needed it, but I'd start learning some of the other work needed in screened garment production. They took me around the whole facility and showed me everything—from the printing presses and the folding and packing station to the darkroom, where they converted art from paper renderings to transparent film sheets. That's where they burned art into the screens through which they'd push ink onto the clothing.

I met everyone who worked for this small company and realized immediately I was the only person of color there. The only Black employee at an all-White business. I wasn't sure how to feel. Less was my concern over that, as my parents raised me to be proud of my race, confident in myself, and accepting of differences in others. More of my focus was that I didn't want to print or fold and pack T-shirts at all. I only wanted to draw. But I was grateful to not have to go back to my previous employment, so I decided not to complain.

I worked there for a few weeks, getting to know the owners, the staff, and the ropes of garment imprinting. I'd hover around Jim's desk and inquire about how he had to design for the best possible print. He was an amazing artist. Our styles were so different. I really liked his work, but I felt like I could add a variety to the offerings if given the chance. Then it came.

One day while folding some finished shirts, one of the owners called me to the reception area. He introduced me to three people who had come in looking for some print work. They worked for a local Christian-based radio station. They had the idea of placing caricatures of their radio personalities above the logo of the radio program they hosted.

The owner asked me to sit down with paper and a pencil to converse with the clients to flesh out the vision they had. Talk about a pressure moment. I was an artist, not much of a people person at 19. But I also saw this as my opportunity: a chance to hook the client with my concept and rendering; a chance to prove I was too valuable to be printing, packing, and doing less creative things. I sat with them—looking them in the eyes as I spoke—and roughly sketched a couple of versions of what they conveyed to me. They seemed to like the direction. Once done, we all shook hands. The owner thanked me for my time, and I went back to the work I was doing in the back room.

Less than a week later, the owners gave me the job of doing the final art for the client. Both owners were very much into their Christian faith, and the client seemed to be one they really wanted to land. I don't think I'd ever taken as much care to draw something with the best of my ability as that artwork. They secured the job, the shirts printed wonderfully, the clients were pleased, and I was happy.

The owners thanked me again and started building a space right next to Jim. I had an art desk, lamp, and all the materials I needed to help produce whatever work came through their doors. I never folded, printed, or swept anything else for the rest of my employment there. I forged a good relationship with Jim as we designed side-by-side until the small business fell on some rough times. They had to lay everyone off and close temporarily.

Things came back around. They reopened the shop and looked to hire back all the same employees. I said yes, but Jim decided to move on to another business. With that, I became the solo artist for Integrity Screen Printers, and we continued to pump out good, quality designs and products. Thank you, Ken, Dave, and Jim, for the clarity of seeing in me what I saw in myself.

CHAPTER 2

CLARITY

Acceptance of what *is* is part one of CLARITY, which is the first C of your journey to becoming a diamond. Part two of CLARITY is picturing what you would like to be, do, or have.

Finding out what you would rather have versus the status quo may prove difficult, but not impossible if you're willing to be clear about where you are. Wiping the mud off your windshield is a wise move before you drive off into the night, right? As Robin Sharma has said, "Vague goals lead to vague results."[2] If you're unwilling to be crystal clear, that's okay for now. As soon as you can, become childlike in your envisioning. Let your imagination explode and allow yourself to create some clarity of the best thing possible.

At the very least, picture something better than now. You want to pair this with a childlike feeling also, not immaturity or foolishness, but strong, emboldening belief. A childlike approach will absolutely help you to visualize that something better. Who has ever stood at the base of a mountain picturing the apex and reached the top with one leaping move? You can picture some greater destination than where you are, or you can picture an incremental step forward. In doing so, take a pause there and begin to feel it. Purposely work to immerse yourself in that feeling of improvement or full manifestation.

The human mind is so powerful, you can do this to the point of engaging your senses, resulting in the feeling of it being done. When your thoughts paint a picture so clearly, then your feelings get strongly behind them, and powers, not fully understood nor explained, come into sync. They do this for the purpose of making your reality match what's imagined. We, the apex species on this planet, have this as our birthright.

Look around you and marvel at all that humans have created. True, we have created horrible realities as well, but they don't outweigh the positive advancements we've achieved. Never has another living thing had the consciousness and desire to challenge, learn, question, and produce as the human species. Show me any animal that has built something to make their existence better than what's provided them by instinct.

If a lion thought to fashion a weapon to disable its prey from yards away, it might find it supremely valuable and do so. It doesn't because it doesn't possess the consciousness needed to do so. We watch and study, capture and release, kill and heal, and preserve lions. They don't invent any devices to help or harm us, to attack better, or to defend themselves greater from humans. Perhaps that's a good thing. Matters not, because they are them, and we are us.

Scientists Gregg Braden and Dr. Joe Dispenza are two of the many who speak of the innate power we have. With much success, they teach many, who adopt and practice how to put the "brain-heart coherence" into play. I practice a lot of their teachings and others'—from religious leaders, gurus, and coaches to motivational speakers and admirable extremists—to gain clarity of some desired things. I am a believer. I continue to practice. It matters not what tactic or whom you follow to gain your clarity, just as long as you do.

REFINING THOUGHTS:
Defining What's Desired

The facts are that many of our life situations won't permit us to easily define what is or what's desired.

We slip, get duped, or simply walk into environments, only to find them uncomfortable, difficult, or downright scary to escape. In those times, we may make the error of justifying why we should stay somewhere we shouldn't be.

We offer defenses, such as *I can't figure a way out. I'm too old now, anyway. It'll be too much work to step backward or start anew. It's always been like this, so what's the point? I don't deserve any better. What would people think?* The list of excuses is as expansive as our imaginations can be. Abusive relationships, self-degradation, illness or unhealthy bodies, financial troubles, and the like are all states that may seem valid for not seeing what is possible.

Sometimes there's a stacking of these occurring simultaneously. Mixing them up can create a cocktail of resentment, depression, anxiety, anger, addiction, hate, or violence. All too often, it seems almost inevitable. What vision of anything greater than the aforementioned states can you pursue without first having the clarity of being in said state? The foundation of all possible change toward the positive is full, unfiltered acceptance of facing absolute truth about what is.

DIAMOND EVOLUTION:
Phase 1

The first phase of four that a rough diamond goes through to become what many admire and find value in is drawing and marking.

This is done to determine how it should be cut to the greatest advantage.

This is the beginning of your quest to become your most valuable self.

Draw a line for yourself that you'll walk to the desired goals. Get a picture as clear as you can imagine of what you want passionately.

Set the mark that you will reach for to become better—for yourself and others.

Writing Your Visions Into Actions

Put your goal(s) to paper so you can visualize them. Draw a line from your current state of health, wealth, love, and/or joyfulness to your desired state between two images or written words or numbers. You don't have to be artistic to create your vision board.

The images can be stick figures you draw, photos of yourself that you print or paste on paper, photos from the web, etc. Or you can write words or numbers—ideally, quantifiable or measurable. Some examples:

Health: weight; blood pressure; glucose level; stress or energy level (scale: 1-10); amount of rest (# of hours of sleep daily)

Wealth: salary (hourly, monthly, annual income); title (new role, promotion); savings, investments, assets; gifts received (count your blessings, and not always just the monetary)

Love: quality time (# of hours/days with family, friends, and/or self); relationship goals (single, married, divorced); spiritual state (# of hours/days of intimate time by yourself or with others: devotion, meditation, prayer, therapy, etc.)

Joyfulness: passions (talents, hobbies, new skills, bucket-list goals); projects or service (# of freelance engagements, volunteer opportunities, giving back); emotional state (time spent laughing, crying, smiling, talking)

Now, place your paper on a wall in a room you will be in each day. You might want to put up an actual board, so you can add more visions as suggested in this book. You might keep more than one wall empty to place pages up (maybe framed or laminated) wherever you'd like all over the room.

If you'd rather not have them displayed on a wall, you might tape them discreetly to the side of your nightstand or collect them all in a binder neatly. Whichever you choose, keep them handy. Make a habit of looking at your visions before you go to sleep.

Once you have clarity of what is and clarity of what's desired (the combined first C of becoming a diamond), the next C must occur to continue toward any better state. This is a pivotal one. I cannot overstate that it's unquestionably necessary.

CHAPTER 3

IN THE DARK

Hello, carbonite. You have the clarity that you are carbon. You also have clarity of being something different, perhaps better, than carbon. Now, you must make an important, possibly urgent, choice: try to remain the same, or move toward what you've pictured? If you choose the latter, that will come with some unknown, uncomfortable experiences. You will be subjected to longer periods of darkness. This will likely be coupled with pressure, even serious pressure.

You will feel the heat, and still, no one may see what you're doing, what you're becoming. But please don't doubt yourself here, because it isn't for them to see. It's not their vision; it is yours. The choice you've made, coupled with the resulting transformation and improvement it promises, is for you. Let your evolution begin. Embrace it.

I mentioned having some artistic gifts earlier in this book, and as my interests moved from field to field, I exercised those talents in various ways. Someone introduced me to a local bookstore owner, and I negotiated a job to illustrate a couple of children's books she'd authored. I created an album cover for a Detroit-based rap group. I made signs for multiple businesses in my city and many others. At age 21, perhaps sparked by working at that great screen print shop, I became really interested in street wear.

During that time, I knew of a few Black designers who were making it big with their brand. They had gained national, if not international, recognition. Many of the hottest rap and R&B performers were wearing their clothing, and I owned quite a few of the well-made outfits they produced. These four young Black men inspired me. I was enamored of the dream they seemed to be living. I pictured entering the same business, so I started sketching my own designs. Eventually, I showed them to some friends and family.

My dad, in a show of support, took me to a trade show held yearly in downtown Detroit. There, I met a guy who worked for this famous brand, which was likely the most popular urban label of the time. I showed him my portfolio with my best designs, and he seemed to like them. While scanning over the renderings, he mentioned that if I were ever in

California, he might be able to get the owners to meet with me.

In my mind, I may have twisted his words into a perceived statement something like, *Come to California, young man, and I'll bet you'll be on your way to becoming the next big name in urban fashion.* Nonetheless, I do recall his words were positive enough for me to feel like I could do something in this field.

I went home excited, believing I could do something spectacular. I thought more seriously about it and created newer, better designs. With each one, I got an exciting, increasing feeling that it would happen for me. How awesome to be a young Black male from Detroit who could end up becoming a wildly popular clothing designer. Seriously, I would go to sleep sometimes picturing my creations on some of the hottest emcees, dancers, and actresses of the day.

By chance, my mom had a brother who lived in Cali. I called my uncle and fully explained my little dream. He listened, then agreed for me to come stay with him and his wife while I gave it a shot. I picked up a second job at a courier company to pay for my plane ticket so I could kick a little money to him while staying there. (Thanks for that suggestion, Mom.)

I stacked my money up, then sought out and found a local seamstress to pay to create one of my favorite designs. I designed a T-shirt as a calling card or "reminder" to hand out to any influential person I might meet. The owners at Integrity even printed my full-color souvenir shirts at no cost. Wow. The plan was set. My family threw a little going-away-follow-your-dream get-together, and many of my friends came by to send me off.

You couldn't tell me this wasn't going to work. I thought, *Go get it, Sivad!*

I went to the front porch one day to retrieve the mail. Mixed in with the other stuff was an acceptance letter from the Detroit Fire Department. I had applied with them more than a year prior, along with the US Postal Service, which my dad and aunt worked for, respectively. It stated that I was to start the academy in a few months. Trouble was, this was during the same time I was set to be in California.

This was a good opportunity, though. My dad had been a Detroit firefighter since I was three years old. Although he never urged me to follow his footsteps in that, I did know it was a career that came with lots of respect and ample time off. Plus, he seemed to really enjoy it. It was a good opportunity, but was it at a bad time?

It wasn't like I was unhappy at all with the life I had. I genuinely enjoyed both of my jobs: drawing for garments the first half of the day, then driving cars (nice ones, like Ford Taurus SHOs, Acura

Legends, and Nissan Maximas) for a courier service. Not to mention they both paid me every week on Friday. Add to that, the latter had multiple stops where a bunch of young, pretty women worked. I always found reasons to lag a bit at those and talk to a couple of cuties. What more could a young single man want?

I had pictured it enough that I really felt my new dream. I was invested mentally and financially. I was thinking, feeling, and acting like it would come true.

Firefighting offered a solid alternative, a sure thing. That created some tough questions to ponder what to do. I talked with my parents about each situation. Eventually they said, "Sivad, you have to make the choice." I still went back and forth over the sure thing and the dream thing. Ultimately, I settled with this: *If I become a firefighter now, I may end up thinking and wondering, What could've, would've, should've happened?*

I decided on going to California. Wisely, my parents suggested writing a letter to the fire department explaining that I appreciated the offer but had to decline. I heeded their advice. The department responded that my application could be put back in the database, and if and when the city was to hire again, I might get a second notification. Well, that was better than a now-or-never response. So, I hopped on the plane when the date came.

DEFINING THOUGHTS:
Seeing Your Choices Clearly

Choosing something for yourself or another can be easy or difficult, depending on what and how many options are available and how you view them. You've likely heard many people say, *I had no choice or I can't decide or It's too hard to pick.*

Look, if you had to eat a poop sandwich, and your choices were human poop or dog poop, albeit on your favorite type of bread (I'll give you that), you'd make a choice. *No, I wouldn't,* you say?

Okay. Well, how about if you were given a third choice? That being, someone with a gun would hold it to your head and pull the trigger if you don't choose and eat a poop sandwich. Are you getting any idea which one of the three options you'd choose?

Now, much less palate-offending and nonviolent would be eating a healthier meal. You could have the home-cooked, heart-carb-smart, or whatever meal that'll do your body some good. Or, you could have a super convenient, flash-frozen, multisyllabic, over-preserved, and processed microwave meal. You've got to eat to survive. Choose, then.

***

My Golden State venture to become the next icon in urban wear didn't play out like my grandiose vision. It wasn't entirely fruitless, though. I did get a meeting with that major brand I admired so much. I remember sitting in the lobby. The woman at the reception desk asked, "How did you manage to get a meeting here?"

I replied, "I just called up and asked."

The look on her face led me to believe that was unusual. I didn't know any better than to just simply ask.

The people I met there ushered me through their building, showed me some of the processes from design to production, and gave me some encouragement and advice. But they weren't looking to back any new designers at the time. They had recently invested heavily in an up-and-coming gentleman from New York. It stung, for real, but I could understand that.

I checked on and stopped by some other brands in California, and one offered me a freelance opportunity with their T-shirt department. Freelance meant if there was steady work coming, I'd get paid. When there wasn't, I'd get no pay at all.

I thought that still might work, so I checked with a cousin first to see what the cost of living was like in California. It was a shocker for me, at 21, that it was so expensive. I decided it was time to go back to Michigan.

Although I didn't get the financial investment or a job I felt would've worked for me, I was satisfied that I chose to go. I figured I didn't want to wonder in my future, What could've, would've happened if I just went for it? I did, so now I knew.

I flew back to Detroit just before New Year's Eve and took a bit of time to myself to reflect on the whole experience. But I knew soon I'd have to get some employment.

During my job search, the US Postal Service sent me a letter to become a carrier. I took it and began delivering mail, but it wasn't the right fit for me. Even though I was earning nice money, I didn't enjoy the work, which led to me not having the best attitude or effort on the job. I considered quitting and even got reprimanded by my supervisor for my lack of the correct work ethic. I wasn't in a good space. For two years while employed there, I felt more and more down.

Then, the Detroit Fire Department offered a second chance to join the academy. The question became Should I keep at this job or run into burning buildings? I jumped at the latter and said yes.

It was definitely different, but I felt energized and grew quickly to love my new career. It was the right move. I've been proudly helping people, making some true friendships, growing as a man, and serving Detroit's citizens for more than 25 years.

When one door closes, another one opens, indeed. I am forever pleased that I went to California. For each of us, in choosing to chase a dream, there is always something we can learn.

CHAPTER 4

CHOICE

The second C to becoming a diamond is: CHOICE. We all have freedom of choice. Always. You shrink or expand, wilt or grow, weaken or strengthen, by your choices. We may live or die by them. Not choosing is in and of itself a choice. As author Toni Sorenson said, "Even indecision is a decision." Don't ever allow anyone to make the most impactful choices for your life when you can. Even with the most difficult matters, the fact is you can choose. Choose.

You have choices: Saving and investing your money, or not. Showing that loved one you care for them, or not. Saying to yourself, "I am enough," or not. Either is an option. Either is a choice you make. You've probably had some instances where your options were so numerous it was hard to even focus on what to choose. This is when a process of elimination would lend itself greatly to your benefit.

Picture all the things available, then start eliminating. You can do this by picking the least favorable one for you. Eventually, you should get down to two options, then prioritize one of them over the other. That is your choice. Another method for making a choice is knowing the difference between what's important versus urgent. It's a prioritization technique, but it works to put things in some order of what goes first, second, and so on. The way I understand it is "important" has to be done, while "urgent" has to be done—right now. With either technique at your disposal, you can make a choice about anything.

If you were in a car that was rolling downhill toward a drop-off, but you also had a deep laceration and were losing lots of blood, you'd have a decision to make. Either stop yourself from bleeding out or stop the car from going over the cliff. Is it clear what you should choose to do first?

Even when things are not black and white, choice is available. We all know each choice we make may not be to our liking or benefit. But our choices create our lives. Past ones brought you to your present state, and current ones will take you to a future state.

Give yourself the permission to make the choice and see where it leads. If you find you don't like where the path is leading you, or where you ended up, make another choice, then follow that path.

REFINING THOUGHTS:
Navigating Life's Mazes

Life is like a series of never-ending mazes, to me. You must enter (if you have life, then you've already entered the first maze) and find your way through. Choose left or right and go, until you hit a wall, then turn around and head in another direction. You do this while remembering your last choice wasn't the correct one.

If you persist, you'll exit one maze eventually, only to enter another. This will go on, until your last day of life.

The mazes can lead through adolescence, young adulthood, maturity, the golden years, etc. There will be mazes for relationships, work, self-discovery, child-rearing, and more.

The practice of exercising choice in each maze entered, including those that don't work out how we'd like them to, strengthen and hone. The result is your ability to make better choices. Don't you want that?

DIAMOND EVOLUTION
Phase 2

Rough diamonds go through a second phase toward becoming a finished gemstone. This phase is the cleaving and sawing process. Here they are split parallel to or against the grain for the purpose of removing impurities or imperfections.

We, too, should seek and choose to walk less-traveled paths and rid ourselves of the things that aren't beneficial while building upon the best of what's within us. We usually do ourselves a great value by going a different route than the majority would take.

It's not for others to see why we make the choices we do. They may find out at some future point why we made the decisions we did, but if not, we still know.

When you recognize something in the distance or deep within that you desire, it naturally feels right to want it. Give yourself permission to choose it—for your growth.

Writing Your Visions Into Actions

Sometimes, we have two choices (or more) to decide between. For the purpose of seeing how to write your visions into actions, think of a choice you need to make that ties into one or more of the goals you have on your vision board. Just pick something for which you only have to decide between two options. Or narrow them down to your final two based on prioritizing between important or urgent.

Draw a line down the middle of a piece of paper. At the top, write down something you have to make a choice between: one option on the left, the other on the right. Sound familiar? Most of us have done this before in some form, often to decide whether to do one thing or not.

On the left, list the pros and cons you envision under this choice in terms of outcomes. In other words, what good might come, and what could go wrong? On the right, do the same. If the pros outnumber the cons on one side, you have clarity now for what is likely the better choice, right?

But what if you have the same number of pros and cons on one side or both? This typically doesn't happen, but it can. If it does, tear off or cover up the cons on each side completely. Now, you only have to compare the positive outcomes between your two choices.

If you found clarity between your choices initially because your pros simply outnumbered your cons greater on one side, well, great. But if you are still having second thoughts, go through the questions below for each "pro" outcome.

STRONGEST:
- Will this outcome strengthen any areas (health, wealth, love, joyfulness) in my life?
- Will this outcome fortify any relationships, plans, or direction for my life?

MOST VALUABLE:
- Will this outcome make me more effective or useful in any areas of my life?
- Will this outcome foster growth or enrich my life and others in some way?

If they are tied, which list has the strongest and most valuable outcomes in your view? Ask yourself the questions again for each pro to get a clearer picture. You might want to answer maybe for some.

Do your best to answer definitively (yes or no) and honestly, for sure.

Which list of pros revealed the most yes answers? Tied again? Go back through and see if you hesitate at all on any. Make any maybe count as a no this time.

You should have more yes than no answers for one choice and find comfort in your gut that this is a clear choice to move you forward.

Now that you've gained your CLARITY and made your CHOICE, it's time to find a promise-worthy thing to pull you where you need to be. You will get profoundly serious with the third C of becoming a diamond.

CHAPTER 5

IN THE MAKING

As the cutting, turning every which way, and reshaping begins toward becoming a diamond, you will feel uncomfortable. You'll feel unsure, perhaps in pain. What did you expect when you made this choice? Just ease, all downhill, zero effort? You thought *no one* would ever see what you're doing, and possibly, probably, say something critical or negative? C'mon now, you rough diamond.

Maybe you could get from beneath the bright light, the magnifying glass, the watchful eye. Perhaps you do hold the power to stop the chiseling of yourself, the pressing against the shaping stone. If you do, go ahead then, make it stop.

Wait. Didn't you promise yourself, or someone else, it was time for a change, for some progress? You committed to be greater than you are now. If you honestly meant it, then remember that. Picture the value you'd like attached to you, the strength you could show to yourself and the world. Envision the light that will shine on and through you that'll amaze those who will glance or gaze at you. Revisit your oath, your gut-level promise, and feel it deeply. Get back to the fire your commitment created.

***

It was a normal workday. That is, if any workday as a Detroit firefighter with all its unpredictability could be normal. I was working at TMS-1, which is short for Tactical Mobile Squad-1. We just called it Squad-1. We were tasked with such duties as providing extra manpower where needed and working the Jaws of Life for vehicle extrications. We also performed fast search and rescue for people reported to be trapped inside a house fire. It was my regular station.

I knew the guys I was working with well as we'd been stationed together for some years. They knew their jobs well, as did I, and we functioned smoothly together. So, when a call came in for a house fire nearby, it seemed the routine would happen. We'd go to the location and do what was needed if it wasn't a false alarm. When the dwelling was extinguished, we'd come on back to the station.

On the way there, a report came over the radio that there were people trapped. Hearing that always increased the tension. Our adrenaline spiked; our heart rates rose. Thoughts of how many people, what ages, and where they might be, ran through our minds. I looked at my friend next to me. Without saying a word, we knew, if needed, he and I would go inside first. That was even before the firehose was ready with some water to attack the fire.

It was early afternoon in the spring, and the sky was bright. The dark smoke we could see rising in the sky was a good indicator we probably had a "working fire" that would require a hose with water to extinguish. Our apparatus didn't carry water. So, it was likely that Engine 59, one of the other two fire companies stationed with us, would be the first company to arrive that could attack the fire. Engine 59 got there first. They went to the closest hydrant and began hooking into it, so their crew could enter the house and put out the fire.

We arrived immediately behind them and noticed a man on the front lawn yelling, "I got out, but my mom is still in there!"

Boom—that was our squad's cue. We were definitely going to enter this home, search for and locate this woman, then bring her out. The front door was closed, but we could see the fire was at the back of the house. There was an open door there, so that was our fastest way in. My buddy and I started putting on our SCBAs (Self-Contained Breathing Apparatus) so we could begin the search. I was ready first. As I entered, another firefighter was ready just before my buddy. So, that firefighter came in between us. It was hot inside—not that there's any such thing as cool fire, but it was a type of heat I hadn't felt before.

I knew to get down on all fours to make my way into the first room. I couldn't see a thing through the thick smoke. I advanced carefully, using my hands and an ax to feel what was before me. My left hand swept the floor, but then hit nothing, and my body lurched forward in response. *Hold up!* I stopped, swept a bit more, and felt a drop-off. I figured it was either a hole in the floor or the stairs to the basement. Not going that way. I backed up a bit and told the guy behind me, "We've got to go another way."

Making our way through the smoke, I heard what sounded like glass breaking. Then I heard a *whoosh,* and a rush of flames entered the room and lit everything up! I dropped flat on my stomach as flames were blowing over my head and coming down the walls around me. I looked behind me, thinking I should go out the way we came in. But I could no longer see the exit, just flames banking down the walls from the ceiling. I knew I couldn't stay there much longer, so I started a military-style belly crawl forward.

I bumped into something, and I stopped in my tracks. I tried to move backward, then forward, but it felt like my air tank was stuck on something, and I was under some obstruction. After a couple more movements, I felt the heat again and got back flat on the floor. I was not sure how long I'd been there, but I realized I didn't see the firefighter who came into the house behind me.

In an odd moment of almost silence, I heard muffled voices coming from outside or somewhere, and I could make out someone saying, "He's still in there. He didn't come back out!"

Could they be talking about me? I'm guessing they are. Maybe I don't know how bad the fire has gotten and, therefore, how bad my situation is. Those are never the thoughts a firefighter wants to have, let alone face.

Situations like this do end up, at times, with the worst possible outcome. I didn't want to get seriously burned in there. I didn't want to run out of air. I didn't want an 11-year career, let alone my life, to end there, flat on the floor of a house in an attempt to save someone. But I briefly pictured that as a possible reality and a heavy feeling followed. A scary, terrible feeling. *Is this my fate?*

DEFINING THOUGHTS:
Pushing Through The Fire

A commitment is like a promise, an oath, or a contract with yourself to be, do, or have what you've chosen. Your commitment, when you make one, should light a fire within you. It should rekindle or fuel that fire whenever things start smoldering, whenever you start slacking or losing your forward action and need to get back on. It should also rage within you when you're grinding on your task toward what you've chosen. This is beyond a simple mental sentiment, beyond something written on a piece of paper, or even stated in front of someone.

The truest commitments should be internal etchings, deep things that speak to you and face you toward that which you deeply desire, like a respected, wise teacher. Or they may grab and yell at your inner being like the most grizzled drill sergeant. You can conceive whatever picture of that type of person you'd like. I'm just saying your commitment keeps you centered and gets you going when you feel like stopping.

If you care at all about what you say, and seeing it through as best as possible, you wouldn't want to give anyone the power, or satisfaction, to see you come up short. You really wouldn't want them to know something worse—that you didn't even try. No way! You have to live with yourself, always.

***

I didn't know how long the fire would be flowing above me, and I wasn't fully sure how much time I had until my air would run out. I couldn't figure how long it would take a crew to come inside with the firehose, or if they'd reach me in time to help. This situation didn't feel good, but I was committed to firefighting, to this squad's work. I was committed to finding this trapped civilian. I was committed to the oath I took when I started this career.

I had even learned the firefighter's prayer. I'd looked especially closely and felt deeply the last line: "And if according to my fate I am to lose my life, please bless with your protecting hand my children and my wife." I wasn't married at the time, but I did have a two-year-old daughter, my first child. *Surely, she'd like to see me come through the door in the morning. I absolutely would like to see her.*

In a flash, I pictured her running to me when I walked through the door, as she had many times before. I saw myself scooping her up, spinning her around, and then diving into her "neck meat" for some tickling. *Is there any better sound than a child laughing uncontrollably from being tickled? She's my "Number One" and I am committed to her, to being her dad.* I committed at that moment to see her tomorrow morning. This instantly became my dominating feeling. *So Sivad, that means you have to get out of this situation and this house—NOW!*

With that, I got back to a crawling position and started bucking and moving every way possible. The floor seemed slippery, but I was moving away from the fire-blocked way I came in. If it's my time to die, it'll be while doing all I can to get out, not lying on the floor. I got free and started moving fast to the next room ahead. When I did, I felt a sort of cool sensation on my face, where my skin was exposed a bit, outside of where my mask ended. I heard scrambling and voices.

Then, I saw a bit of daylight. *Is that a window or an open door in front of me?* It was actually the Engine crew, and they had made it inside. That sensation must've been some of the smaller spray from the firehose they carried. *Thank goodness we met up, and they didn't hit me full blast!* I may have startled them as I rushed forward, but I was just grateful I was about to get out of there.

I made my way through the front door and onto the porch. I snatched my mask off, taking in a big gasp of fresh air. Someone in the driveway noticed it was me and yelled, "He's here! Sivad is on the front porch!"

I made eye contact with my boss and let him know I was okay. Then I asked if anyone found the woman yet. He responded he didn't think so.

I put my mask back on and jetted back in the front, behind the crew I just passed on my exit. I felt way more confident—with them headed toward the seat of the fire—to begin searching for the stairs to the second floor. I don't recall if that's exactly what the man on the front lawn had said, but I had noticed there was a second floor when we arrived. So, that's where we picked up the search.

I did find the stairs and told the firefighter closest to me I was going up. They followed. At the top of the stairwell, we were met by extreme heat and very dark smoke. Not surprising, given the fact that heat, smoke, and flames seek the highest point. What mattered was doing the quickest, most thorough search we could do to find her before the conditions worsened and it became problematic for us as well.

I suggested we split up so we could search all rooms faster. The first one I entered had some furniture in it. So, I swept the floor with my hands, making my way through, and patted down anything that felt like a bed. Nothing there. I went back in the hallway and yelled out, "Did you find anything?" He said no.

I went into the next room and performed the same type of search. When I patted down what seemed to be a bed, I felt what was possibly a foot. I swept up, down, and to the right, finding what I thought was another foot. Immediately, I moved upward to confirm it was a body.

I yelled, "I got one!" Then, I grabbed the person underneath the armpits and dragged the body off the bed and into the hallway just as the other firefighter met me at the door. We carried the person down the stairs and quickly recalled that the son, and quite possibly some neighbors, could be out front. So, we took the person out the back door. A couple of firefighters outside saw us and signaled for the EMS workers to bring their stretcher. We laid the body on it, and they whisked her down the driveway, but not before I could see her. She was very tiny, wearing a nightgown or something, and was covered in soot from head to toe.

My wishes were that she was going to be all right, and I knew we'd done all we could do for her.

All the work wasn't finished, because the fire had to be completely extinguished. We'd also do a thorough search to make sure no one else was inside. It all got done. We packed every piece of equipment up and started heading back to our station. On the ride back, my crew asked me what happened inside, as I asked them the same from what they saw outside.

It appeared that some windows broke, introducing a bunch of fresh oxygen into the house, which caused a flashover, an instant rush of fire into a space, in the room I was in. I had been temporarily trapped in the table and chairs of the kitchen/dining area.

Realizing it hadn't turned out bad for me, the light, albeit twisted, sense of humor of firefighters resumed. One of the guys said, "I'm glad you're okay, Sivad. But if you hadn't made it, I hope you wouldn't have been upset with me eating your lamb chops." *Ha! Me too.*

CHAPTER 6

COMMITMENT

The third C of becoming a diamond, as you can clearly guess, is COMMITMENT.

Commitments shouldn't be small and light. They should be big and monumental in the importance of making them, even for small things. The step of making them should pull you toward their completion.

Build yourself to setting bigger commitments, if you must, by the practice of living up to your smaller, singular ones. When the pride of accomplishing what you've committed to grows, you can dare to go bigger, maybe even scarier.

To go through life having never made a commitment to any worthwhile thing shouldn't be called a life at all. Just call it existence.

REFINING THOUGHTS:
Committing To Be All You Can

I believe all other living things, creatures, and plants come into being with "commitments" to be all they can. As Jim Rohn noted, a tree grows as tall as it possibly can[3], regardless of when it's been pruned, battered by elements, or even affected by fire, if given the opportunity.

Watch ants as they spill out of their hill to find and consume a piece of food someone dropped. They are all committed to the mission at hand of biting their own piece off and carrying it back to the colony. If something or someone steps down on them, surely a great deal will be killed. But the ones that survive and are able will move around the wounded and dead to get to their portion and move toward the destination. That's commitment.

You could be just as determined as the singular tree or individual ant, just as driven, having made a promise to yourself to get what you envision. Or, you could say it, and with the thought of a proverbial shoe coming down or placing one down yourself, you leave it as just words. Instead, you waffle, wince, woe-is-me, and wiggle your way into nonaction. See how close you get to what you choose that way.

Commitments hold those who take them seriously to the line. They rarely, if ever, will go against them for anyone, including and especially themselves. It could be like taking the podium before millions and making a promise to do, or not do, something—then allowing those millions to follow you daily afterward watching, quick to remind, *What about your promise? I thought you were going to back up your words.*

DIAMOND EVOLUTION
Phase 3

Phase three in diamond processing is bruting, which is the shaping of the base. It's where the diamond receives its form. Bruting can be done manually, but it's mostly done mechanically now. Sometimes, even a laser is used for this work.

The commitment you set may involve manual work, perhaps lots of it. In one form or another, some mental work will be necessary, or a combination of the two.

Without a doubt, additionally and likely most importantly, your commitment will involve heart work. If your heart isn't in your work, it will show; that is, if you perform any work at all.

Whether the work you've promised to do can benefit from mechanical help, or lasers, like bruting (shaping) of some kind, will depend on what you're committed to. Either way, make and stick to your commitments to build your base and take on the shape of what you envision.

Writing Your Visions Into Actions

On a new blank piece of paper, write down that choice you decided to make in Chapter 4 based on the outcome of your pros and cons lists, and make it more visible.

First read and then follow these directions:

1. Start at the bottom center of the page and draw a hand with a finger (or an arrow, if easier) pointing upward.
2. Write a short description of the choice you made above the finger or arrow.
3. Draw a hand with a finger (or arrow) pointing upward above the choice.
4. Then, write a statement of your commitment to that choice above the finger or arrow.
5. Draw another hand with a finger (or arrow) pointing upward above your commitment.
6. Next, write two or more of your "yes" outcomes from your "winning" pros list as sentences (centered) to form a paragraph.

7. At the top center of the page, write the heading, "I AM BECOMING A DIAMOND" in all caps, and below it, write the subheading "The Strongest, Most Valuable Version of Me".
8. Customize any wording in the brackets shown below as you see fit, and your page should end up looking something like this, but larger:

I AM BECOMING A DIAMOND
The Strongest, Most Valuable Version of Me
This choice I have decided to commit to will strengthen my [health, wealth, love, and/or joyfulness] in life. It will also fortify my [plans, relationships, and/or direction] for my life. This commitment will foster growth in the most valuable ways.
☝
I have committed to [doing what?].
☝
I will [describe your choice:
9 words max].
☝

If you are skilled in art, graphic design, or simply formatting documents, your words might form a perfect diamond shape. If it looks more like a heart, perhaps intentionally (artwork is heart work) or a V (maybe for vision or victory), that is perfectly fine, too. If the alignment is slightly or completely off, no stress. Again, this vision is just for you. The purpose is to be intentional and committed to your goals.

You can make four "diamond" commitments to place on your walls, one for each area (health, wealth, love, and joyfulness) in your life, if one choice doesn't cover all four. Or you may choose to concentrate on one area at a time. Just don't overwhelm yourself with too many goals simultaneously. And remember to celebrate—even the smallest victory—as you achieve them and move on to the next.

CHAPTER 7

IN THE LIGHT

If not now, soon you'll take stock of where you are, and realize how far you've come. You've endured complete darkness, withstood incredible heat, and survived amazing pressure. You're close now to a new, improved state. Each positive thought, every good feeling, and all forward action moves you toward that state. Stay consistent in these three.

You will reach a point of strength that none can deny, a level of brightness that no one can dim, and an increased value that few, if any, could foresee. You saw it, though.

When you reach a milestone, acknowledge it to yourself. It's okay to congratulate yourself on even your smallest advance. Regardless of who started, assisted, or supported you along this path, it would not have happened if you didn't adopt a reason why you should do it.

Definitely thank those who played part in your successful journey, but be sure to include yourself in the thanking. If you're too modest to do it aloud, say it mentally. There is no reason to stop either. A quote by John Henry Newman goes, "Growth is the only evidence of life."[4] You can and should set another goal once you achieve the last one. Consistency is a big part of the way.

***

The musical ringtone on my obsolete cell phone sounded, and I got out of bed to shut it off. It was the first one to two minutes of Rick Ross's "Hustlin'." It was 6 a.m. I sat back down to gather my thoughts. I glanced at the wall near the foot of my bed and saw it—the chart. The chart I taped up the night before to record my first month of cold showering.

It was March in Michigan, so the water was certainly cold. Not as cold as in January, but not as warm as, say, July. *Wait, "warm" cold water? What am I thinking?* I shuddered at the thought of getting in there. Why did I think to do this?

I recalled that I was skimming social media and ran across a guy nicknamed The Iceman. Wim Hof is a big promoter of cold exposure and its benefits. He claimed that using his method, one can influence the autonomic nervous system, boost the immune system, and experience other potential health benefits.

He also implied humankind has become ill-adapted to the cold through our progression, comfort, and technology.[5] Basically, he was saying we're soft as a species (my words, not his). I had already read about other high performers in sports, business, and different fields singing the praises of taking a brisk, cold shower for better focus and so forth.

I looked into it, read about the science, individuals' different opinions, testimonials, and takeaways. I had watched numerous videos and techniques, and finally decided, Why not? I'd been running into burning buildings exceeding 600 degrees for more than 20 years. So how could 15 seconds of cold water be any more of a threat to my body? Plus, if it benefited any of them, perhaps it could me.

My personal pep talk was working well until I realized that everyone, every single person I had been researching, was White. I am Black. I thought, *Is there a reason I didn't see anyone of my color doing this? I don't think I should try it. I really don't have to try this.*

Chiding myself, I rebutted, *What was the purpose of watching all the different videos, downloading the app, printing a chart, and setting the timer on your phone?* I even grabbed a red Sharpie marker to check off the five days a week, as suggested, to do this.

It's just a couple of months, I reasoned. *So, either you're going to do it, or not. You said—not to anyone else but yourself—you would. And if you're going to do it, then do it. Today!*

DEFINING THOUGHTS:
Doing The Work – Repeatedly

If you get clarity about a situation you realize you're in, and you get clarity about some better situation you'd prefer to be in, good! Then, if you make a well-thought-out choice to have that favorable situation become your new one, great! Furthermore, if you make a true commitment to get there, awesome!

None, absolutely none of that will even matter if you don't begin and, more importantly, continue doing the work of getting to your desired state. When I say work, I mean any kind of work necessary to get there. Physical, emotional, educational, spiritual, financial, mental, or more—there are all types of work that must be done, repeatedly.

Picture people standing at the base of a mountain. They have the clarity of where they stand and the vision of being at the apex of that mountain. Now, they've chosen to get there. They've gained the know-how, geared up, and developed a plan to ascend it. They've committed themselves to the task, and if serious, embodied the feeling of pride they'll have once placing their flag at the top of this mountain.

All that doesn't mean a thing if they don't start climbing and continue until the point they've desired to reach is met. This can be done, even allowing for breaks, reevaluation, redirection, or more.

As noted earlier, not one of them can simply take one powerful leap and reach the highest point of the mountain or any other. So, if they get there, they must employ the fourth and final C of becoming a diamond: CONSISTENCY.

CHAPTER 8

CONSISTENCY

Without CONSISTENCY, you can complete nothing. Not even the most common, taken-for-granted task, such as putting your own pants on, will occur. You have to picture them being on, decide you'll have them on, commit to putting them on, and then take all the necessary, sequential actions to have them on—correctly, if you care about that sort of detail. Consistency, in any matter, brings about the end result.

I have spoken on the "feeling" in the context of each of the previous three C's within this book. Feeling is most certainly in consistency. As you're going through the steps, stages, phases, or whatever it'll take to get what you truly desire, there must be a feeling to accompany your consistent actions.

"FEEL LIKE IT" is a statement I printed in big capital letters on a piece of paper and placed in my room in 2018. I often found myself looking at it during the times when I didn't want to do any number of things: doing a workout or stretching routine, journaling, having a difficult conversation, setting an appointment, recording a video and more.

Seeing and reading those words didn't solicit a demand, but more of a call to what it would be like to have done whatever I said I would or set out to do. Looking at those three simple words got me through many of these helpful tasks when I thought of not doing them.

I highly recommend you read diverse literary works, in whatever form, that speak directly to the importance of how you feel about something affecting your experiences in life. Digest and make the writings a staple to your self-development efforts to aid you in crafting a life with purpose.

I am not saying, by any means, you'll always feel like staying the course or following the steps to acquire what you desire. I am saying that if you don't discipline yourself into being consistent, then all your thought, talk, planning, and promising will be just empty rhetoric. You'll have only yourself to blame.

Forward steps—even the smallest, even those not in the straightest line—if made consistently, will get you to any goal. Picture how close you'll be to that goal versus not remaining consistent. How else do we believe—logically thinking, that is—we'll reach our goals?

REFINING THOUGHTS:
Being Consistent For Growth

Teleporting to the top of Mount Everest isn't possible. A one-move leap to the end of a 26.2-mile race won't happen. Attending one class on cash flow principles doesn't ensure our financial freedom. Sitting in lotus pose a singular time and uttering "ohmmm" can't bring us eternal peace and enlightenment. Lifting any amount of weight—one rep, one time—will not earn us the physique we envision. Walking the aisle and stating our wedding vows isn't a single step to solidify an enriching, marital relationship. You get what I'm saying?

Each of these desirable outcomes—after the other three C's—requires your CONSISTENCY.

I must tell you some—no, much—of what you'll have to do consistently, few if any will see. Do not let that deter you one bit. You're not going to do what you must do to prove anything to anyone but yourself. As I decided to tell myself, many solo times, after having done the consistent work, *Sivad, it's not to announce to anyone, 'I told you so.' It's to say, 'I told*

ME so' to the only person I'll have to live with, until I transition: myself.

An amazing feeling washes over and strengthens you when you tick off those consistent actions, knowing you're growing, and growing closer to whatever you've focused on and sent your energy toward.

***

I turned the water on warm at first, stepped into the shower, and then gradually turned it down until it was cold. No doubt, in Detroit in March, cold water is *col-l-l-ld* water! That 15 seconds was taking forever. Then the timer's end sounded. I felt like I could jump through the curtain to the outside of the shower.

Looking in the mirror, though, I was like, *Okay, Sivad. Systems check. I'm awake, wide awake, for sure now. Check. I have some goose bumps but not frostbitten. Check. I have some major shrinkage. That had better not last. But hey, who's gonna know that?* (I guess everyone who's reading this now.) The main thing is, I did it. I dried off, grabbed my main phone to record it on the app, and then went to my room to the chart.

With the red Sharpie in hand, about to make the notation of having completed day one, I decided to make a "commitment mark" instead of a check mark. The letter *I*. It happened to be that the five blank spaces per week were exactly enough for me to write in, "I-D-O-I-T." I did it because I said I would. So, if I did it today, I can surely do it tomorrow.

I woke up the next morning and repeated the process, adding the next letter, then increasing the time. A week of 15 seconds became 30 the next, then 45, then 60. I got brazen and upped it to two minutes before I heard a voice, perhaps my in-head drill sergeant, saying, "You've been keeping a bit of warm water on this whole first month. Either commit to doing it—no cheating—or stop it altogether!" *Build my base, sir? Take on my shape, sir? Sir, yes, sir!*

I ticked each day my second month and moved to all seven days per week at two minutes, zero warm water. I made it to the warmer months, then committed to going a whole year (plus made up the month that I cheated myself). When telling my dad about it, he asked, "How long have you gone?"

I said, "Six minutes, one time."

He said, "Wow! That's close to 10."

So, the next morning, I did 10. While listening to a motivational YouTube video, I heard a speaker describe discipline as doing 11, when someone else stops at 10. It was like a challenge, a challenge accepted. So, I did 11 minutes.

I took advantage of the winter as December rolled around and did my cold exposure outside in about four inches of snow. My youngest watched from the window as I stood there in only a pair of basketball shorts. I decided to lie in it face down, then on my back, and make some snow angels to delight her. She yelled through the window, "You're a crazy man!"

I realized I could do this. I enjoyed the clarity and focus it gave me after each shower. I was dialed in to the morning, feeling like I could accomplish anything. I'd only been sick three days total in that whole 365 days. *I'll take it.* I started waking up at 5 a.m. daily since then and taking a cold shower to benefit from that practice. "Win the morning, win the day," as the saying goes. Crazy man? Nah. But I am a better man from my consistency, for sure.

DIAMOND EVOLUTION
Phase 4

The final phase of four in diamond processing is polishing. This gives the diamond its facets. The most popular has 57 to 58 facets and is called brilliant. Brilliant!

What a thing to be stated. Wouldn't it feel great to be called that? To look at yourself and confidently say that? Of course, it would. You can, you should. Say it now, "I am brilliant!"

Say it as much and as often as you'd like. It will give you what many lack—what they need, which is so vitally important—the feeling. The feeling of shining brightly like a diamond.

If at some future point, you find yourself feeling dull or lackluster, know this: You are still a diamond. You just require some polishing to regain that shine.

Writing Your Visions Into Actions

Take note of how your new surroundings affect your life. How do your diamond visions affect your dreams? Are you waking up with hope or excitement for achieving them? Are they moving from dreams to reality? If so, move them around on (or off) your vision board or wall or wherever you're keeping them.

Maybe you want to create an "Achieved" side on your board or wall to place them as you move to your next goals. Maybe you want to collect them in an "Achievements" binder you can flip through to see and appreciate your accomplishments and growth.

Always remember to celebrate your victories, even those you consider small. Make time to write down your positive thoughts, good feelings, and forward actions with consistency (daily, weekly, monthly, or as they happen). Some examples:

POSITIVE THOUGHTS
"I had a dream last night that I achieved..."
"I had a daydream that I succeeded in..."
"I am thinking about starting a [new business or health regimen] focused on..."

"I am thinking of becoming [the next or the first person to] ..."

GOOD FEELINGS
"I feel really good about the outcome of ..."
"I feel good about my conversation with [whom] today about ..."
"I feel great about my [decision to do or relationship with] ..."
"I feel good about the [clear direction revealed or path opened] for me to ..."

FORWARD ACTIONS
"I am going to shine in my health goals by ..."
"I am [becoming wealthier/being blessed] by ..."
"I am going to love [myself/others] more by ..."
"I am filling my life with joy by ..."

CHAPTER 9

IN CONCLUSION

Now, to state something quite plainly, I've written none of these words to proclaim that anyone's journey will be quick in process or identical to anyone else's. My process worked for me. It was mine alone. Your process, your excursion, will differ.

The four C's of becoming a diamond are what I've condensed, through my extensive searching, trying, adjusting, and learning. I've had many letdowns, as you've read, and flat-out failures along the way. But I've had positive experiences and full victories as well.

Everything I have ever been through contributed to where I am and who I am. I wouldn't change a thing because I know it would change my current state in life. I am grateful for my life. Life is better than the alternative.

I speak sincerely on feeling within this work, because I understand that without feeling, nothing is created. I practice now what so many throughout time have practiced to their benefit, as well as countless others; that is combining defined thoughts with lifted emotions.

The greatest thoughts, ideas, and visions are just subjective until elevated, persisted-upon feeling comes into correspondence. Then and only then does it become objective in the world. Please believe this.

Becoming a diamond through the four C's—CLARITY, CHOICE, COMMITMENT, and CONSISTENCY—works. Employing the proper thoughts, feelings, and actions to each C works, absolutely.

We get one time in this experience called life, which we all must leave, and none of us knows when we'll go. My desire for you, the reader, is to take on that which is necessary to make yourself and, subsequently, your experience memorable and worthwhile.

I honestly believe something exceptional can come from something common, given the right conditions, work, and enough time. This Instant Means Everything. Start investing your TIME to create the strongest, most valuable version of you.

Start becoming a diamond.

NOTES

1 **Jordan B. Peterson,** "Censorship on Campus | Taking the lead on freedom of expression," session at the 2017 Manning Center Conference in Ottawa, Ontario, CA, February 23-25, 2017, posted by Canada Strong and Free Network on April 6, 2017, YouTube video, 40:52. https://www.youtube.com/watch?v=30U1AAuo_wE.

2 **Robin Sharma,** "5 Rituals That Predict Success," YouTube video, 04:33, December 15, 2016, https://www.youtube.com/watch?v=LxXZ-7W1dBM&feature=emb_logo.

3 **Jim Rohn,** "Wake Up Your Potential," motivational speech, Facebook post. https://www.facebook.com/OfficialJimRohn/posts/10151470566675635.

4 **John Henry Newman,** Newman's summary of a doctrine of the biblical scholar Thomas Scott (1747–1821), Apologia pro Vita Sua (1864) 'History of My Religious Opinions from 1833 to 1839.' Oxford Essential Quotations, 4th ed., Oxford University Press, published online, 2016. https://www.oxfordreference.com.

5 **Wim Hof,** "Wim Hof Method Benefits: Discover the potential health benefits of the Wim Hof Method," Innerfire BV, https://www.wimhofmethod.com/benefits.